Going on a Airplane

Bee Social

ISBN: 9798862107906

THIS BOOK BELONGS TO

_____

HEY THERE, LITTLE ADVENTURER!

ARE YOU READY TO GO ON A FANTASTIC JOURNEY?
BUCKLE UP BECAUSE WE'RE ABOUT TO DIVE INTO
A SPECIAL STORY ALL ABOUT TAKING A TRIP ON AN
AIRPLANE. YOU SEE, AIRPLANES ARE LIKE MAGICAL
BUSES IN THE SKY THAT CAN TAKE US TO THE MOST
INCREDIBLE PLACES! BUT GUESS WHAT? THIS ISN'T JUST
ANY STORY – IT'S A SUPER-DUPER SPECIAL MISSION
TO HELP YOU BECOME AN EXPERT AT FLYING AND
MAKE YOUR AIRPLANE TRIPS SUPER FUN AND COMFY.
SO, GRAB YOUR IMAGINATION, PUT ON YOUR TRAVEL
SMILE, AND LET'S SOAR INTO A WORLD WHERE
FLYING IS NOT JUST ABOUT REACHING NEW PLACES
BUT GOING ON AN INCREDIBLE ADVENTURE AND
HAVING A GREAT TIME!

GOING ON AN AIRPLANE IS AN EXCITING ADVENTURE.

SUN	MON	TUE	WED	THU	FRI	SAT
			1	2	3	4
			3	4	5	6
7	8	9	10	11	12	13
14	15	16	17	18	19	20
21	22	23	24	25	26	27
28	29	30	31			

PEOPLE PLAN AIRPLANE TRIPS FOR LOTS OF REASONS. TAKING AN AIRPLANE IS A GREAT WAY TO VISIT FAMILY OR FRIENDS THAT LIVE FAR AWAY OR JUST TO TAKE A SUPER FUN VACATION.

ONE OF THE FIRST THINGS YOU DO TO PREPARE FOR YOUR TRIP IS PACK YOUR SUITCASE.

IT WOULD HELP IF YOU ONLY PACKED WHAT YOU NEED, BUT REMEMBER TO TAKE SOME COMFORT ITEMS LIKE STUFFED ANIMALS, TOYS, BOOKS, OR MOVIES.

WHEN YOU ARRIVE AT THE AIRPORT, YOU NEED TO CHECK YOUR LUGGAGE AND PICK UP YOUR BOARDING PASS.

SOMETIMES THE LINE IS LONG AND SOMETIMES THE LINE IS SHORT.

YOU MAY GET SCARED OR EXCITED, BUT DON'T RUN OFF.

YOU NEED TO STAY WITH THE PEOPLE YOU CAME WITH SO YOU DON'T GET LOST.

THE AIRLINE STAFF IS VERY FRIENDLY AND WILL HELP YOU CHECK IN AND GET YOUR BOARDING PASS.

THEN YOU WILL GO TO THE AIRPLANE GATE.

BUT FIRST, YOU WILL NEED TO GO THROUGH THE SECURITY CHECK.

THE SECURITY OFFICERS WILL CHECK YOUR BAGS.

YOU WILL HAVE YOU PUT YOUR SHOES, PHONE, AND OTHER STUFF YOUR POCKETS IN A BASKET. THEN, IT WILL GO THROUGH THE X-RAY MACHINE.

YOU WILL ALSO WALK THROUGH A SPECIAL MACHINE, BUT DON'T WORRY IT DOESN'T HURT.

THEN YOU PUT EVERYTHING BACK IN YOUR POCKETS AND PUT BACK ON YOUR SHOES.

THE AIRPLANE GATE IS WHERE YOU WILL GET ONTO THE AIRPLANE. YOU COULD SEE SOME AIRPLANES.

IT MIGHT TAKE A WHILE SO SIT QUIETLY AND READ A BOOK OR PLAY A GAME.

DON'T RUN OFF; IT IS VERY CROWDED, AND YOU CAN EASILY GET LOST.

WHEN IT IS TIME TO BOARD THE PLANE, YOU MUST WAIT YOUR TURN.

THEN, YOU GET TO WALK DOWN A TUNNEL TO THE AIRPLANE.

WHEN YOU GET ON THE PLANE, YOU MIGHT SEE THE PILOT. THEY SIT IN THE FRONT OF THE AIRPLANE.

WHEN YOU GET INSIDE THE AIRPLANE, YOU WILL NEED TO FIND YOUR SEAT.

THE SEAT NUMBERS ARE LISTED ABOVE ALL THE SEATS.

THEN YOU PUT YOUR LUGGAGE IN THE OVERHEAD CARRIER.

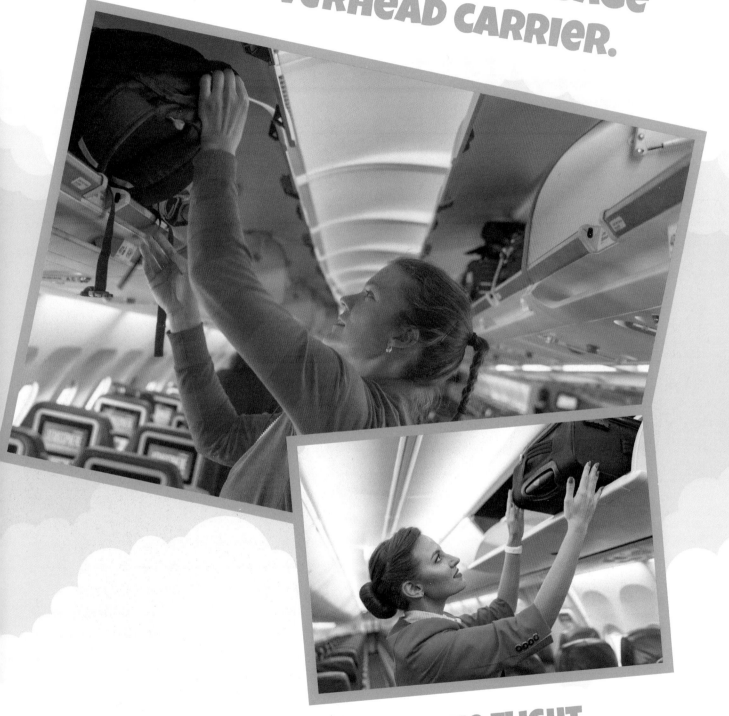

YOUR PARENT OR THE FLIGHT ATTENDANT CAN HELP YOU.

YOU CAN ALSO BRING A LITTLE BAG OF TOYS, BOOKS, STUFFED ANIMALS, SNACKS OR GAMES AND PUT THEM UNDER YOUR SEAT SO YOU CAN GET TO THEM DURING THE FLIGHT.

THEN, REMEMBER TO FASTEN YOUR SEATBELT.

YOU CAN ASK THE FLIGHT ATTENDANT IF YOU need ANYTHING OR HAVE A QUESTION.

THE FLIGHT ATTENDANTS WILL THEN MAKE SURE ALL THE OVERHEAD COMPARTMENTS ARE CLOSED, AND THEN THEY WILL GIVE A SAFETY SPEECH.

AS THE PLANE STARTS TO TAKE OFF, YOU MIGHT FEEL SLIGHTLY NERVOUS.

BUT REMEMBER THAT AIRPLANES ARE VERY SAFE.

DURING THE FLIGHT, THE FLIGHT ATTENDANTS SERVE SNACKS AND DRINKS.

Remember To Say "Please" And "Thank You" When They Give You Your Snack.

You Can Also Bring Your Own Personal Snacks Onto The Plane.

WHEN THE SEATBELT SIGNS ARE OFF, YOU CAN WALK AROUND THE PLANE.

BUT DON'T RUN AROUND, SCREAM, OR BUG OTHER PEOPLE.

WHEN THE PLANE IS FLYING, YOU CAN READ A BOOK, PLAY A GAME, OR EVEN WATCH A MOVIE.

YOU CAN ALSO LOOK AT THE CLOUDS FROM THE WINDOW OR NAP.

THERE IS even A TOILET on THE AIRPLANE IF YOU MUST GO TO THE BATHROOM.

WHEN THE AIRPLANE STARTS TO LAND, YOU HAVE TO SIT IN YOUR SEAT WITH YOUR SEATBELT ON.

WHEN THE PLANE STARTS TO LAND, YOU MIGHT FEEL A LITTLE PRESSURE IN YOUR EAR.

IF YOU YAWN, BLOW YOUR NOSE, OR CHEW ON SOME CANDY, IT WILL GO AWAY.

WHEN THE PLANE LANDS, YOU MUST WAIT PATIENTLY UNTIL IT IS TIME TO GET OFF.

IF YOU NEED HELP, YOUR PARENT OR THE FLIGHT ATTENDANT WILL HELP YOU.

THE LAST THING YOU DO IS PICK UP YOUR LUGGAGE AT THE BAGGAGE CAROUSEL.

FLYING ON AN AIRPLANE IS A LOT OF FUN AND A GREAT ADVENTURE.

PREPARATIONS BEFORE THE FLIGHT

MARK THE DATE ON A CALENDAR

Hang a calendar with a marked departure date a few weeks before travel.

INVOLVE YOUR CHILD IN THE TRIP PLANNING

Explain to your child where they will be going, who they will see, and what they will do. Try showing them pictures or videos.

SOCIAL STORY

In the weeks leading up to your trip, read this social story with your child that overviews the air travel process.

PRE-PACK MEALS AND SNACKS

A limited assortment of foods may be offered in the terminal or on the airplane.

EXERCISE BEFORE DEPARTURE

Traveling on an airplane involves extended periods of being quiet and sitting still.

PLAN AHEAD FOR YOUR SEATS

Consider requesting bulkhead or aisle seats, particularly if your child likes to kick their legs or move around.

COMFORT ITEMS

Pack necessary coping or treatment items in your carry-on bag, like a change of clothes, toys, blanket, favorite toy, game, headphones, or plane-safe electronics and medicines.

ROLE-PLAYING ALTERNATIVE

Role-playing at home is an adequate alternative if your airport does not allow for an actual practice run in the facility or for you to take photographs or videos.

VISUAL SCHEDULE

Kids with autism benefit from knowing what to expect, especially when faced with routine changes.

REWARD CHART

Put together a reward chart and list what rules and behaviors are expected.

ARRIVE EARLY

It would help if you arrived early at the airport to allow for unexpected delays.

PLAN FOR THE UNEXPECTED

Air travel during the holidays often has delays or cancellations. Have contingency plans for possible flight delays. Start checking your flight a few days before. Review departure gates and make sure you know how to get to connecting gates.

ACCOMMODATIONS

PROTECTIONS

The ACAA and the Department's disability regulation, 14 CFR Part 382, protect individuals with disabilities in air travel.

ACCOMMODATIONS

Some airports offer desensitization tours, which allow you to visit the airport ahead of time to help your child get used to the crowds, sights and sounds. Contact your airport for more information.

Call the airline before your flight asking for accommodations.

- Preboarding is offered for children and their families.

- Bulkhead seats or seats with extra room are available. They offer greater leg room and room for a child to soothe themselves.

- Most airlines will do their best to accommodate any special requests as long as they are made in advance.

AIRPORT SECURITY

Travelers requiring special accommodations or concerned about the security screening process at the airport may ask a TSA officer or supervisor for a passenger support specialist who can provide on-the-spot assistance.

ON THE AIRPLANE

BOARDING

Notify the gate attendant that you are traveling with a child or a child with ASD, and you will be allowed to board early or last, depending on your preference.

EAR-POPPING

To prevent discomfort in the ears during takeoff and landing, preemptively encourage your child to suck on a piece of candy or chew a piece of gum. If your child is unable to suck on candy or chew gum safely, a chewing toy can also be effective in reducing ear-popping.

WATCHING THE TIME.

Placing a digital clock or a countdown timer in front of your child may help them know how much longer they can expect to be in flight.

IN-FLIGHT ENTERTAINMENT

Allow your child access to items in their travel bag (See "Before the flight"). Allow your child access to DVDs, iPods, books, coloring books, toys, etc. If your child enjoys tactile stimulation, they may benefit from playing with play dough or putty while on the airplane.

CONGRATULATIONS!

YOU HAVE EARNED YOUR HONORARY PILOT WINGS.

Printed in Great Britain
by Amazon

43283562R00023